IS IT
science?

# Astrology and Astronomy

Rebecca Stefoff

Cavendish
Square

New York

Published in 2014 by Cavendish Square Publishing, LLC
303 Park Avenue South, Suite 1247, New York, NY 10010

Library of Congress Cataloging-in-Publication Data

Stefoff, Rebecca.
Astrology and astronomy / by Rebecca Stefoff.
  p. cm. — (Is it science?)
Includes index.
ISBN 978-1-62712-506-2 (hardcover) ISBN 978-1-62712-507-9 (paperback) ISBN 978-1-62712-508-6 (ebook)
1. Astrology — Juvenile literature. 2. Astronomy — Juvenile literature. I. Stefoff, Rebecca, 1951-. II. Title.
BF1708.1 S83 2014
133.5—dc23

Editorial Director: Dean Miller
Senior Editor: Peter Mavrikis
Copy Editor: Cynthia Roby
Art Director: Jeffrey Talbot
Designer: Amy Greenan
Photo Researcher: Julie Alissi, J8 Media
Production Manager: Jennifer Ryder-Talbot
Production Editor: Andrew Coddington

The photographs in this book are used by permission and through the courtesy of: Cover photo by John Davis/Stocktrek Images/Getty Images; Landolfi Larry/Photo Researchers/Getty Images, 1; Beverley Vycital/E+/Getty Images, 4; DETLEV VAN RAVENSWAAY/Science Photo Library/Getty Images, 6; CORNELL CAPA/Time & Life Pictures/Getty Images, 8; Stocktrek Images/Getty Images, 9; Larry Keller, Lititz Pa./Flickr/Getty Images, 10–11; Forster Forest/Shutterstock.com, 12; SCIENCE SOURCE/Photo Researchers/Getty Images, 14; Baris Simsek/E+/Getty Images, 16; AP Photo/Sang Tan, 17; Fototeca Storica Nazionale/Photodisc/Getty Images, 20; Photo Inc/Photo Researchers/Getty Images, 21; NYPL/Science Source/Photo Researchers/Getty Images, 24; akg-images/Newscom, 25; William Herschel at work at Observatory House, Slough (colour litho), Cameron, John (1830-76) (after)/Private Collection/The Stapleton Collection/The Bridgeman Art Library, 26; © Bettina Flitner/laif/Redux, 28; Dorling Kindersley/Dorling Kindersley/Getty Images, 29; © AP Images, 30; Natal Chart – Adam/GNU Free Documentation Licencse, 31; AFP Credit: AFP/Getty Images/Getty Images, 32; © Stapleton Collection/Corbis, 33; © AP Images, 34; USGS/ Mars-Schiaparelli/USGS Astrogeology: Martian Hemesphere Image, 36; Andreas Cellarius/The Bridgeman Art Library/Getty Images, 38.

Printed in the United States of America

IS IT
science?

# Contents

Ancient people called the band of
glowing light across the night sky
the "Milky Way." Today astronomers
know that is made up of the stars of
Earth's home galaxy.

# It All Started with Stargazing

Thousands of years ago, **astrology** and **astronomy** were the same thing. Each started with people stargazing, or watching the night sky.

Many cultures around the world knew every detail of the heavens. They knew where to find the brightest stars, how those stars wheeled across the sky each night and changed with the seasons, and where the sun's path crossed the sky at different times of year.

They also saw that a few bright lights didn't move with the rest of the stars but followed their own patterns. These were the planets Mercury, Venus, Mars, Jupiter, and Saturn, which were big enough to see with the human eye. The planets too small to see—Uranus, Neptune, and Pluto—were discovered later. (In 2006, the International Astronomical Union moved Pluto to a group called "dwarf planets," bodies in the solar system that are smaller than planets but larger than asteroids, and that don't orbit other bodies the way moons do.)

**The eight planets of the solar system and their orbits, with the Milky Way in the background.**

Knowledge of the heavens had practical uses in people's everyday lives. At the same time, the heavenly bodies were linked to ideas about gods, goddesses, and fate. People believed in a connection between what happened in the sky and what happened on Earth. If events on Earth matched the movements of heavenly bodies, then people who could predict those movements could predict earthly events as well. This was the origin of astrology and astronomy.

Sometimes there was a clear difference between **astronomers**, who studied the movements of the planets, and **astrologers**, who told what the movements meant. More often, the person who studied the skies was both an astronomer and an astrologer. People did not see a difference between the two.

Then, in the seventeenth century, the **scientific method** came into use. The scientific method is a way of testing ideas about the world to find out if they are true. It made the differences between astrology and astronomy clearer.

# ONE

# Science, Real and False

**S**cience is the search for accurate knowledge about the world and how it works. The scientific method is a set of directions to guide that search.

## The Scientific Method

The scientific method is a process, or series of steps. There are many versions, but the basic steps are:

*Observation*

*Research*

*Hypothesis*

*Test or Experiment*

*Conclusion*

*Share and Repeat*

*Observation* means seeing something that raises a question. For example, in 2011 America's space agency, the National

Aeronautics and Space Administration (NASA), reported that pictures of Mars showed dark streaks running down some hillsides. Astronomers asked, "What are those streaks?"

*Research* means gathering data or information that might answer the question. Maybe the answer is already known. If it is not known, research gives the scientist data that may lead to the answer.

To answer their question about the streaky Martian hills, NASA astronomers started their research by looking at many

**Astronomer Gerard Kuiper (1905-1973) preparing to photograph Mars through a telescope at McDonald Observatory in Texas.**

pictures of Mars. The astronomers learned that the streaks appeared in spring and summer, disappeared in winter, and returned the next spring. The streaks looked a lot like the trails made by water flowing downhill. But the scientists already knew the temperatures on Mars. Some streaks were in places so cold that water could not flow. It just froze. The streaks couldn't be water—so what were they?

A *hypothesis* is the next step in the scientific method. It is an educated guess based on what the scientist has observed and researched. NASA astronomers came up with a hypothesis for the dark streaks on Mars. The streaks could be caused by flowing brine, or salty water, which stays liquid at colder temperatures than pure water. NASA called the flow of brine "the best explanation for these observations so far."

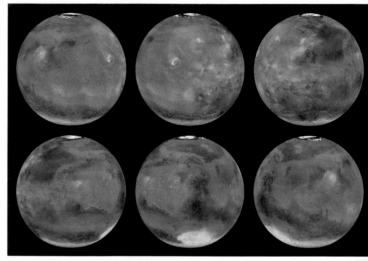

**Ice caps on Mars shrink at the north pole (top row) in February, but at the south pole (bottom row) they reach their largest size.**

*Testing* the hypothesis shows whether or not it is the right explanation. This part of the scientific method usually involves experiments. To test their briny-water hypothesis, NASA scientists could set up a laboratory with temperatures like those on Mars. They could build slopes matching the angles and soil of the Martian hillsides. Then they could pour different liquids, including brine, down the slopes to see whether they leave streaks like those on Mars. Another test would be to send a robotic probe to the surface of Mars to take samples from the streaks and analyze them.

A *conclusion* comes from tests and experiments. In this step, the scientist looks at the results of the experiments and asks, "Do these results support my hypothesis?"

If the answer is "no," the scientist adds the results to his or her observations, then thinks of a new hypothesis. Good scientists admit their mistakes and wrong ideas, because their goal is to be accurate and truthful. Good science is also flexible, growing and changing as new knowledge is gained.

If the answer is "yes," the scientist usually *repeats* the experiment to make sure. To be considered scientific, the result of a test or experiment must be able to be duplicated in exactly the same way. Scientists *share* their work by publishing it in **scientific journals** so that others can also test it and apply the results to their own research.

### Full Moon? Forget About It!

Once every 29.5 days, the moon is full. Its glowing, silver circle is beautiful—but does it drive people and animals crazy? For hundreds of years people thought it did. That's why *Luna,* the ancient Roman name for the moon, became the word *lunatic,* or insane person.

Some people still believe that accidents and crimes are more likely during full moons, or that hospitals and police are extra busy on those nights. Television shows and movies call this the "full-moon effect." But researchers using the scientific method have not been able to prove that the full-moon effect is real.

Take the example of dog bites. A study of English hospital records in the 1990s showed that people's chances of being bitten doubled on full-moon days. However, an Australian study at the same time found that dog bites did not increase during full moons. Researchers have looked for the full-moon effect in crime, accident, and medical records. No solid proof has been found.

The scientific method is a powerful way to learn about the world. It gives scientists everywhere a clear set of standards to meet. It is also an excellent tool for identifying **pseudoscience**.

## Pseudoscience

*Pseudo-* (SOO-doh) at the beginning of a word means "false" or "fake." Pseudoscience is false science. It is presented as if it were scientific, but it does not meet the standards of good science.

Pseudoscience makes broad claims. An astrologer might say, for example, "People with the astrological sign Aquarius care about the human race." This claim is so broad that it can't

The scientific method says that for a hypothesis to be accepted, the results must be able to be repeated. "The full moon changes behavior" is a hypothesis. But repeated tests have led to different results, not to agreement. So why do people believe the full moon causes odd behavior? The scientific answer is called **confirmation bias**.

Confirmation bias means that people notice and remember things that fit into ideas they already have. If you've heard of the full-moon effect and you fall off your bike on the day of a full moon or read about a crime happening that same night, you might think, "Well, of course. It's the full moon." But if the accident or crime happened some other time, you wouldn't think, "Hey, it's not a full moon today."

Maybe people *have* done strange things during a full moon. Before there were flashlights and electric lights, the full moon may have led to mischief, just because it lit up the night.

**Sometimes a newspaper
horoscope seems "so true."
What about the other times?**

be tested. Just about everyone cares about "the human race."

Pseudoscientific claims are vague. In astrology, claims often take the form of predictions based on **horoscopes**, charts that show the position of the sun and planets in the sky at a certain time. Most predictions are not very detailed. "You will come into money soon" could mean almost anything: finding a nickel on the sidewalk, getting your allowance or paycheck, or winning a million-dollar prize.

Claims might also contradict each other, or say opposite things. One astrology website says that people with the sign Aquarius like fame *and* privacy, two things that don't usually go together. The same website calls Aquarians "good communicators" *and* "tactless"— another contradiction.

Pseudoscience appeals to feelings and hunches instead of logic and reason. Someone might read his or her horoscope and say, "That sounds like me!" instead of asking, "Could this apply to a lot of other people I know?"

Maybe you've read your own horoscope and thought, "Exactly right!" That moment makes a powerful impression because of confirmation bias. We notice confirmations (things that agree or seem true) more than we notice refutations (things that don't

## Science or Pseudoscience?

| FEATURES OF SCIENCE: | FEATURES OF PSEUDOSCIENCE: |
|---|---|
| • Based on scientific method | • Often based on tradition or folklore |
| • Uses reason and logic | • Appeals to feelings |
| • Looks for physical forces to explain results | • Explains results in mystical or mysterious ways |
| • Testable | • May not be testable |
| • Results can be reproduced | • Results cannot be regularly reproduced |
| • Published in scientific journals, and for the general public, too | • Published for the general public, sometimes does not meet standards of scientific journals |

agree or that seem false). In other words, most people give more weight to "hits" than to "misses." It's easy to be impressed when a horoscope "comes true" or seems accurate. To avoid confirmation bias, we have to pay equal attention to statements that are meaningless, untrue, or inaccurate.

Pseudoscientific claims are sometimes presented as facts but with no evidence. If there *is* evidence, it may be statistics or quotes with no **sources**. Without knowing exactly where a piece of information comes from, it's impossible to check that the source is reliable and that the information is accurate.

Everyone agrees that astronomy is scientific. What about astrology? To answer that question, it helps to know something about what astrologers and astronomers do.

## Astrology and Astronomy

***An Astrologer Casting a Horo-scope,*** **from a 1617 book by English astrologer and mathe-matician Robert Fludd. The blue globe shows the heavens as seen from Earth.**

**TWO**

# Astrology and Astronomy: What's the Difference?

"**W**here were you born? When? Do you know the exact time?" If you go to an astrologer to have your horoscope made, be ready to answer those questions.

### What an Astrologer Does

An astrologer uses the positions of the sun and planets to understand things about people and events on Earth. Astrologers work by making horoscopes that show where those heavenly bodies are, or where they were in the past—at the moment you were born, for example.

Horoscopes are supposed to predict what is going to happen to you, tell you something important about yourself, or answer questions. Maybe you've seen them online or in magazines.

They appear in sets of twelve, and they look something like this:

*LEO (July 23–August 22):*

*Watch your words today. If you communicate badly, someone*
*close to you may misunderstand you. An exciting chance will*
*come along if you are ready to try something new.*

If horoscopes are easy to find, why would someone go to an astrologer? And why would the astrologer need to know exactly where and when the person was born?

The horoscopes you see in magazines or on websites are called **sun sign** horoscopes. There are twelve sun signs in a year, each about a month long. Everyone born between July 23 and August 22, for example, shares the sun sign Leo.

Sun sign horoscopes are pretty simple. They don't go into much detail. How could they? Each horoscope is supposed to be true for one-twelfth of the people in the world!

To make a more detailed, personal horoscope, an astrologer goes beyond the sun sign. Using the position of the sun and planets at the time a person was born, the astrol-

**The twelve signs of the zodiac are the basis of sun sign horoscopes.**

oger makes a horoscope, also called a birth chart. Explaining the meaning of a birth chart may fill many printed pages. Some astrologers draw birth charts the old-fashioned way, with pens and colored ink. They use shelves of reference books to spell out the meaning of each symbol. Others use computers with astrology software.

Astrology is ancient. Cultures around the world have practiced it over the centuries. Millions of people still believe that some unknown force from the heavenly bodies is linked to people and events on Earth. But millions of others see astrology as **superstition**, an old idea that doesn't make sense and isn't scientific.

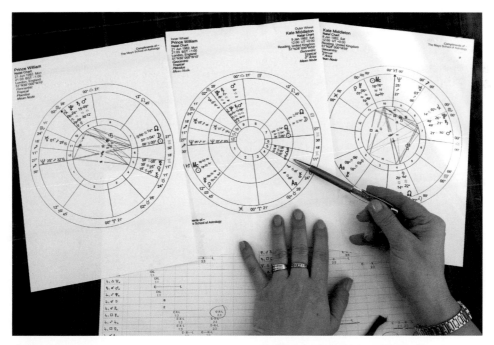

**Before the wedding of Britain's Prince William and Kate Middleton in 2011, British astrologer Wendy Stacey made these birth charts of the couple. Astrologers predicted a happy royal marriage.**

Is astrology "real"? Can knowing where Mars was when you were born really tell you what's going to happen in your life? One way to answer those questions is to compare astrology with astronomy.

### Who Believes in Astrology?

In 1994, a poll found that 37 percent of Americans, or more than one in three, were believers. A 2009 poll showed that the number of believers had dropped to about 26 percent of Americans, or one in four. Is this drop just a brief trend, or is astrology losing followers for good? No one knows—not even astrologers.

## What an Astronomer Does

*Astrology* and *astronomy* sound a lot alike. That's because they come from the same root, the Greek word for "star."

Like the astrologer, the astronomer looks to the sky for answers to questions. But astronomers ask different questions. Instead of wanting to know what will happen in their own lives, they are curious about how the universe works. They study the sun, moon, planets, and stars to learn about those heavenly bodies, not to learn about themselves or events on Earth.

Astronomy is the study of space and everything in it, from the closest heavenly body, the moon, to the farthest galaxies. It is a science, which means that it follows the steps of the scientific method. At one time, astronomy was thought to be the same as astrology. The story of how they split apart is, in many ways, the story of science.

# THREE

# The Big Split

In the ancient world, knowledge of the heavens was a survival tool. People looked at the sky to find their way around and to tell time. They also believed the skies held information about life on Earth.

## Practical Uses of Sky Watching

Knowing what the sky looks like at different times of the day, night, and year is useful for navigating, or getting from one place to another. Simply knowing how to tell directions by the sun can get a person home. By measuring the position of the sun and stars, sailors and explorers found their way across the world's oceans. Even more importantly, they found their way back again!

Timekeeping was another use of sky knowledge. Ancient peoples traced the circular path that the sun seems to follow against the background stars. The path is called an ecliptic, and the band of sky along the ecliptic is called the **zodiac**. One complete trip of the sun around the zodiac is a year. People divided

**By knowing the movements
of the heavenly bodies,
ancient astronomers
could foretell certain
events, such as eclipses
of the sun and moon.**

the year into months based on the
changing appearance of the moon,
which goes from full to new (or dark)
and back to full every 29.5 days.

## The Oldest Star Map

In ancient China, astrology and
astronomy were one. Sky watchers
there started keeping records of sun-
spots, eclipses, and meteor showers
around 2,500 years ago. They also
mapped the night sky. In 1907, a set
of thirteen sky maps was discovered
in a cave in Dunhuang, China. Made
around the year 700 AD, these maps
form the world's oldest star atlas.
They accurately chart the positions
of more than 1,300 stars. Astrological predictions for each section of
the sky are written on the maps.

## Planet Power

From early times, many peoples thought that events on Earth
were shaped or decided by the heavens, believed to be the home
of gods and spirits. The ancient Babylonians identified the plan-

ets with gods and goddesses. Mars was linked to Nergal, god of war. Venus was the planet of Ishtar, goddess of love and growth. The Greeks, Romans, and Norse later shared these ideas about the planets and the gods.

As ancient astronomers kept detailed records of the heavenly bodies' movements, they saw patterns that let them predict those movements. Some astronomers could even predict eclipses, rare events in which the sun or moon seems to disappear for an hour or so. Imagine how impressed a king must have been if his chief astronomer declared that at noon on a certain day, the sun would turn black—and then it happened!

## Astrology Rules

Some astrologers were powerful, respected figures in society. Emperors, kings, and generals asked for their advice. Astrology guided all kinds of decisions, from what day to start building a temple to whether an army should go to war. Ordinary people had questions, too. They asked astrologers for insight on matters such as getting married and choosing a name for a newborn child.

Astrology as practiced in Europe and later in America is called Western astrology. It remained strong for many centuries. In the sixteenth century, Queen Elizabeth I of England had a court astrologer, as did most other rulers. Europe's top scholars studied astronomy *and* astrology.

### Magellan's Astrologer – Smart Guess, or Did He Read It in the Stars?

Explorer Ferdinand Magellan was the leader of the first Europeans to sail around the tip of South America and into the Pacific Ocean. When Magellan set out with five ships in 1519, he took an astrologer named Andres de San Martín. Months later one of Magellan's ships, the *San Antonio,* failed to return from a scouting mission. Magellan asked the astrologer what had happened. San Martín told him that a pilot named Estêvão Gomes had mutinied, seized the ship, and headed back to Spain.

Magellan and the others kept going. Two years later, after sailing around the world, the survivors returned to Spain. There they learned that everything San Martín had said about Gomes and the *San Antonio* was true.

Had the stars told San Martín what happened?

Maybe. Another possibility is that San Martín simply understood human behavior. Not only had there already been one mutiny before the *San Antonio* disappeared, but Gomes had complained about Magellan and urged the expedition to turn back.

San Martín probably didn't need the stars to tell him that Gomes seized the ship and had gone home. But the astrologer did not predict the mutiny, and he failed to warn Magellan of another important fact about the voyage—that Magellan would die in the Philippines before he could complete the first trip around the world.

Starting in the seventeenth century, astronomy and astrology began to separate. Astronomy gradually became the science we know today, while astrology fell somewhat out of favor.

## New View of the Heavens

The early Greeks practiced astrology, but they also tried to understand the universe using scientific tools such as mathematics. The scientific quest took a huge leap forward in the early seventeenth century when a new invention, the telescope, gave people a closer look at the heavens.

Suddenly, the moon was no longer a silver disk in the sky. It was a world with mountain ranges like those on Earth. The planets were worlds, too, with moons of their own. And there were more stars in the sky than anyone had seen before the telescope existed.

**Regiomontanus was a famous astrologer, astronomer, and mathematician in fifteenth-century Germany.**

Seventeenth-century astronomers proved what some earlier ones had claimed: Earth is not the center of the universe with the sun, moon, and planets all revolving around it. Instead, Earth moves like the other planets, all revolving around the sun. This new view of the universe shook up people's ideas, but it was just the first of many astronomical surprises.

In 1781 English astronomer William Herschel did something for the first time in human history. He discovered a new planet that could be seen only through a telescope. It was named Uranus. Astrologers had to scramble to fit Uranus into their systems of planetary influences. They did the same thing in 1846, when the planet Neptune was discovered, and again in 1930 for Pluto.

Meanwhile, astronomical discoveries kept coming. The band of stars known as the Milky Way turned out to be a galaxy, an enormous spiral of stars. Our sun lies on the fringe of one of its arms. Beyond it

The invention of the telescope let people see the heavenly bodies more clearly, launching a new era of scientific astronomy.

## The Pluto Problem

In 2006 the International Astronomical Union, made up of many of the world's astronomers, voted to "demote" Pluto from planet to dwarf planet, one of many small worlds orbiting the sun. Suddenly the solar system only had eight full planets, not nine. But although astrologers had squeezed Pluto into their systems in 1930, most modern astrologers refused to kick it out. "Whether he's a planet, an asteroid, or a radioactive matzo ball," one astrologer said, "Pluto has proven himself worthy of a permanent place in all horoscopes."

William Herschel, the first person to discover a new planet, draws an astronomical diagram in his study. One of his giant telescopes can be seen through the window.

are billions of other galaxies with uncountable trillions of stars. The universe is bigger, older, and more complex than the stargazers of the ancient world imagined.

Astronomy is helping us explore the universe with deep-space probes, satellites, and a vast variety of telescopes. But what about astrology?

**Astronomer Eva Grebel at work
in the Astronomical Calculation
Institute in Heidelberg, Germany. She is an expert in the
subject of how galaxies form.**

# FOUR

# Astrology and Astronomy Today

**A**stronomers today are busy discovering planets around distant stars, measuring the speed of galaxies, and watching stars being born from clouds of glowing gas. Closer to home, they are sending spacecraft on missions to explore our solar system in more detail.

Astrologers remain busy, too. In many parts of the world, astrology is part of daily life. In India, for example, many parents turn to astrology for help in naming their children. They often start projects, such as opening a new business, on a day that an astrologer has said will be lucky or successful.

In the Western world, the rise of science—especially astronomy—pushed astrology to the sidelines until the 1960s, when the hippie movement began. Hungry for new ways of looking at the world and themselves, many people turned to one of the oldest ways: astrology.

At that point, astrology started being less about predictions and more about **psychology**. Instead of foretelling the future, astrologers offered people a tool for understanding themselves and others. Some astrologers even claimed they could help people find love by telling them which sun signs matched their own.

## Astrology and Politics

Five hundred years ago no European king or queen would have been caught without a royal astrologer. Even popes sought astrological advice. In the Western world, astrology remains popular, but it no longer has the high respect it once enjoyed. When news broke in 1988 that U.S. president Ronald Reagan and his wife, Nancy, had secretly been bringing an astrologer to the White House for years, many Americans were shocked and alarmed that the country's leader took astrology seriously.

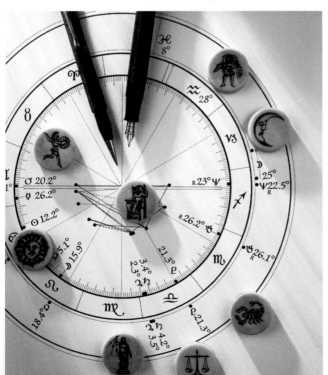

## Astrology: Science or Not?

For thousands of years, people believed that celestial objects made things happen on Earth. A person's character and life events were shaped by the planets in the houses of the zodiac at the time of his or her birth. Many astrologers today

**An astrological chart with discs showing signs of the zodiac.**

**Astrologer Joan Quigley made headlines for her link to President Ronald Reagan in the 1980s.**

have a different idea. Heavenly bodies do not *cause* earthly events. Instead, the heavenly bodies are *signs* that mirror earthly events. These signs can be interpreted.

Some astrologers don't see what they do as science. For them astrology may be a spiritual practice, or the art of uncovering hidden knowledge, or foretelling the future. In this view, astrology draws on forces or abilities that can't be fully explained.

Other astrologers insist that what they do *is* science. It follows laws that can be explained, and it deserves respect from the scientific community. Some have even gone to court to prove their case. In 2004, the Supreme Court of India ruled that astrology is a science and could be taught in the nation's universities. If astrology is real, some connection must exist between the planets and events on Earth. What physical force could provide that connection?

Gravity is the force that holds the planets in their orbits and moves the oceans up and down with the tides. But tides are caused by the gravitational pull of the moon, which plays very little part in astrology. The planets are so far away that their gravitational effects are barely felt on Earth. They are more affected by the gravity of closer objects. According to astrologers, the planets affect newborns at the moment of birth. But when a doctor delivers a baby, the mass of the doctor's body has six times more gravitational force on the newborn than the planet Mars has. That force is so weak that the newborn doesn't feel it! The gravitational force that nearby people and objects have on newborns has no effect on them and isn't claimed to shape their character, so how could the much weaker gravitational force of distant planets do so?

Electromagnetism (EM) is the force that creates magnetic fields. The sun's electromagnetic field reaches Earth, peaking whenever there are storms or flares on the sun. Most of the planets have magnetic fields, too, but their effect on Earth is tiny compared to that of the sun. Yet

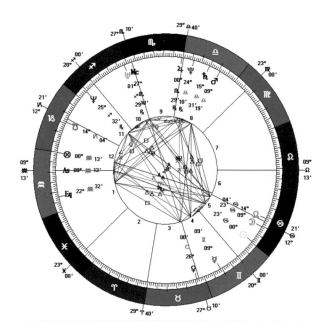

A birth chart produced by astrology software.

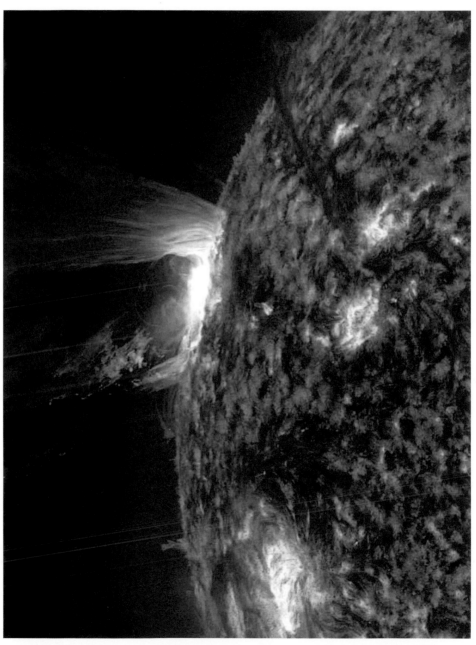

An eruption on the sun sends waves of electromagnetic energy (EM)
toward Earth. The planets, in contrast, have almost no EM effect on Earth.

Indian astrologer Savita Thakkar explains some
of her predictions in 1999. One of them was
that World War III would start in early 2000.

astrologers give much more importance to the planets than to the sun. Like gravity, EM does not explain how the heavenly bodies, other than the sun, could be linked to earthly events or people's personalities.

## Putting Astrology to the Test

If astrological effects are real, they should be able to be measured using the scientific method. Since the middle of the twentieth century, believers and critics have performed many tests. Overall, the results have not been good for astrology.

One of the first serious tests of astrology was done in the 1950s by a French psychologist named Michel Gauquelin. He used the birthdates of athletes, politicians, journalists, and other successful people to get their horoscopes. Gauquelin wanted to see if there was a connection between people's achievements and the positions of the five traditional planets at the time of birth.

Gauquelin found a connection. Sports champions had a higher-than-average chance of having been born with Mars in certain parts of the zodiac. The same was true for military leaders with Jupiter, and for artists with Venus.

After Gauquelin published his results in 1955, his findings became known as the "Mars effect." If Gauquelin was right and the Mars effect was real, then the planets were linked to individual personalities, abilities, and lives in a way that could not be explained by chance alone.

More than half a century later, experts still do not agree on whether Gauquelin *was* right. His work set off a long controversy. Investigators argued that Gauquelin's research methods were flawed, but others defended him. Various researchers have tried to reproduce Gauquelin's results. Some found small evidence of a Mars effect. Some found none. Each of those studies started *new* arguments.

**Is the "Mars effect" real?**

Most scientists today think the Mars effect is pseudoscience. Other tests of astrological claims have fallen short as well. In one study, researchers looked at people who were born at the same time in the same place, but were not related. According to astrology, these "time twins" had identical birth horoscopes. Their personalities and lives should have been more similar than chance would allow. But the researchers found no such similarity. Another study tested astrologers' abilities to describe people's personalities based on birth horoscopes.

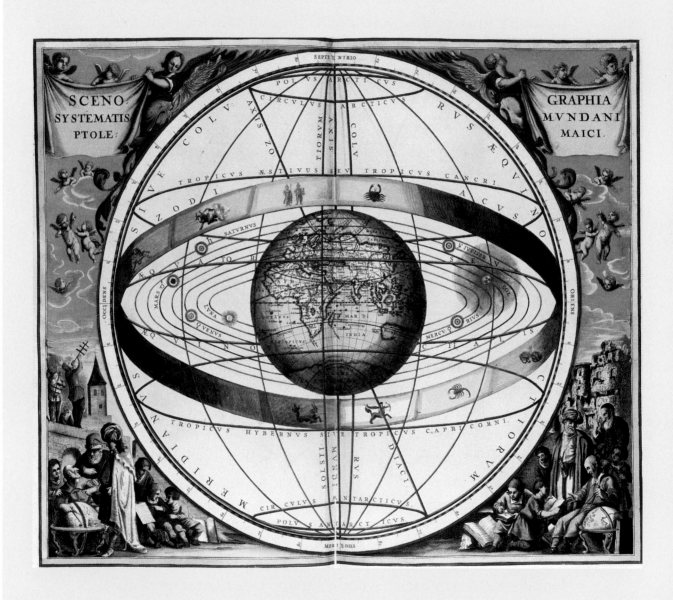

German mapmaker Andreas Cellarius published a large star atlas in
the seventeenth century. This page shows the constellations arranged
along the zodiac band.

## Test Astrology Yourself
## You can test astrology with simple experiments.

Find a horoscope for any sign of the zodiac. You may choose Taurus, for example. Remove the sign and the dates so nothing shows that the horoscope is for Taurus. Make copies.

Ask six or more friends or fellow students to tell you their zodiac signs. (Be prepared to look up signs by birth date for people who don't know theirs.) Tell them that you are going to give each person a copy of his or her horoscope. Then hand out the copies you made of the Taurus horoscope with identifying clues removed. Don't let them see each other's copies or read the horoscope out loud.

Ask them individually to rate how accurate "their" horoscope is. How many think it is "somewhat" or "very" accurate? How many of those people are Tauruses, if any? How many are surprised to learn that they all received the same horoscope?

Find a horoscope for each of the twelve zodiac signs. Remove all identifying clues, so that no one knows which horoscope goes with which sign. (Keep a master copy for yourself, so *you* will know.) Make multiple copies of each one.

Give the whole pile of horoscopes to six or more friends or fellow students. If possible, give them to people you haven't used as test subjects before. Ask everyone to pick out the horoscope that fits them best. How many pick out their actual zodiac sign?

For all of your experiments, keep records of your test results. Analyze them. What conclusions do you reach? If you can repeat the experiments with a larger number of people, are the results the same or different?

Astronomers follow the age-old practice of studying the heavens in this image from a seventeenth-century map of the constellations.

The astrologers' results were no better than chance.

The bottom line: no solid scientific proof of astrology has yet been found.

## Two Branches from the Same Root

Astronomy and astrology were once the same, but for hundreds of years they have been separate. One is a scientific tool for learning about the universe around us. The other is a way of looking at life and the world that gives comfort, entertainment, or food for thought to millions of people, but doesn't meet the standards of science.

If you were going on a mission to Mars, who would you want to plan your take off: an astronomer or an astrologer? Most people would want an astronomer in charge—but some might check with an astrologer, too, just in case.

# Timeline

| | |
|---|---|
| **by 2000 BC** | Sky watchers in several cultures record astronomical observations |
| **1600s AD** | Telescopes give people a new view of the heavens; the scientific method comes into use |
| **1781** | Discovery of the planet Uranus |
| **1846** | Discovery of the planet Neptune |
| **1907** | Oldest-known star atlas, made around 700 AD, discovered in China |
| **1955** | Michel Gauquelin announces the "Mars effect," claiming that the planets influence people's lives; other researchers criticize his methods |
| **1960s** | Interest in astrology is reborn in the United States and Europe |
| **1988** | News breaks that U.S. president Ronald Reagan and his wife consult an astrologer |

| | |
|---|---|
| **1990s** | Studies of the "full-moon effect" produce conflicting results |
| **2004** | India's supreme court says that astrology can be taught as a science |
| **2006** | Astronomers decide that Pluto is a dwarf planet, not a planet |
| **2009** | A poll finds that 26 percent of Americans believe in astrology, down from 37 percent in 1994 |

# Glossary

**astrologer**　　　someone who creates horoscopes by
　　　　　　　　using astrology

**astrology**　　　　the act of making horoscopes; based on the
　　　　　　　　belief that the positions of the sun, moon,
　　　　　　　　and planets contain information about
　　　　　　　　people's lives, or answers to questions

**astronomer**　　　a scientist who studies space and the
　　　　　　　　things in it

**astronomy**　　　the scientific study of space and the
　　　　　　　　things in it

**confirmation bias**　the tendency to notice or give more weight
　　　　　　　　to results that confirm or support an idea
　　　　　　　　than to results that do not support an idea

**horoscope** an astrological chart that shows where the sun, moon, and planets are located in relation to the stars at a specific time, such as the time of someone's birth (also called a "birth chart")

**pseudoscience** false science; something that looks like science, or claims to be science, but isn't

**psychology** the study of the mind and how it works; also, the practice of helping people with mental problems or questions

**scientific journal** a magazine with articles written by scientists; before appearing in a journal, an article must be approved as scientific by a panel of experts

**scientific method** a set of practical steps for answering questions about the world and adding to knowledge

**source**     details about where a piece of information comes from so that others can check to see whether the source is reliable and that the information is repeated accurately

**sun sign**     the part of the zodiac where the sun appeared to be when someone was born

**superstition**     a belief or habit that is not logical or reasonable and may even be disproved by science; may be based on belief in luck or magic

**zodiac**     a band or zone in the heavens along the path that the sun appears to follow; astrologers use various zodiacs, but all are divided into twelve sections called houses; for about a month each year, the sun is in one of those houses

# Find Out More

**Books**

Carey, Stephen S. *A Beginner's Guide to Scientific Method.* Independence, KY: Wadsworth, 2011.

Crawford, Gregory. *Animals in the Stars: Chinese Astronomy for Children.* Rochester, VT: Bear Cub Books, 2002.

Driscoll, Michael, and Meredith Hamilton. *A Child's Introduction to the Night Sky: The Story of the Stars, Planets, and Constellations—and How You Can Find Them in the Sky.* New York: Black Dog & Leventhal, 2004.

Glass, Susan. *Prove It! The Scientific Method in Action.* Oxford, UK: Raintree, 2006.

Kerrod, Robin. *Universe.* New York: DK Children's, 2009.

Lippincott, Kristen. *Astronomy.* New York: DK Children's, 2008.

Miles, Lisa, Alastair Smith, and Judy Tatchell. *The Usborne Book of Astronomy and Space.* London: Usborne, 2010.

Mitton, Jacqueline. *Zodiac: Celestial Circle of the Sky.* London: Frances Lincoln Children's Books, 2008.

Stefoff, Rebecca. *Prophets and Prophecy.* New York: Marshall Cavendish Benchmark, 2008.

**Websites**
**How Science Works**
http://kids.niehs.nih.gov/explore/scienceworks/index.htm
Part of the National Institute of Health website, How Science Works is designed for kids and includes a summary of the scientific method.

**A Brief History of Astronomy**
http://cass.ucsd.edu/archive/public/tutorial/History.html
A University of California at San Diego professor gives an overview of how the science of astronomy has developed since ancient times.

**History of Astrology**
www.astrologers.com/history
The American Federation of Astrologers provides a short overview of the history and different forms of astrology through its section. "Astrology: Fact or Fiction?"

# Bibliography

The author found these sources especially helpful in researching this book. A complete list of sources is on her website, www. rebeccastefoff.com, under Sources>Astrology or Astronomy.

Berlinski, David. *The Secrets of the Vaulted Sky: Astrology and the Art of Prediction.* New York: Harcourt, 2003.

Curry, Patrick. *Prophecy and Power: Astrology in Early Modern England.* Princeton, NJ: Princeton University Press, 1989.

Dean, Geoffrey. "The Mars Effect and True Disbelievers." *Skeptic.* Last modified April 6, 2011. http://www.skeptic.com/eskeptic/11-04-06/#feature.

Gauquelin, Michel. *The Cosmic Clocks: From Astrology to a Modern Science.* Chicago: Regnery, 1967.

Hester, Jeff, Bradford Smith, George Blumenthal, and Laura Kay. *21st Century Astronomy.* New York: Norton, 2010.

Kelly, Ivan W. "The Concepts of Modern Astrology: A Critique." *Psychological Reports,* 81. Last modified 2005. http://

www.astrology-and-science.com/a-conc2.htm.

Lewis, James. *The Astrology Encyclopedia*. Detroit: Gale Research, 1994.

Newman, William R., and Anthony Grafton, eds. *Secrets of Nature: Astrology and Alchemy in Early Modern Europe*. Cambridge, MA: MIT Press, 2006.

Roach, John. "**Full Moon Effect on Behavior Minimal, Studies Say.**" *National Geographic News*. Last modified 6, 2004. http://news.nationalgeographic.com/news/2002/12/1218_021218_moon.html.

Seymour, Percy. *The Scientific Basis of Astrology*. New York: St. Martin's Press, 1992.

Willis, Roy G., and Patrick Curry. *Astrology, Science, and Culture: Pulling Down the Moon*. Oxford, UK, and New York: Berg, 2004.

# Index

# About the Author

**Rebecca Stefoff** has written many books for young readers on
a variety of subjects such as science, exploration, history, literature, and biography. Her books about science include the
four-volume series Animal Behavior Revealed, numerous books
about animals and biology, and a biography of Charles Darwin.
She has also probed the mysteries of the unexplained in the
five-volume series Secrets of the Supernatural (Marshall Cavendish Benchmark, 2008). Two astrologers have made detailed
horoscopes for Stefoff based on the time of her birth. Both horoscopes are about half right and half wrong, but in different ways.
Stefoff lives in Portland, Oregon.